First published in 2015 by
The Solopreneur Publishing Company Ltd
Cedars Business Centre, Barnsley Road, Hemsworth, West Yorkshire WF9 4PU
www.thesolopreneur.co.uk

Printed in the U.K.

For further copies, please go to - www.theblinks.co.uk.
Also available on Kindle.

Dedication

To all Parents.
You are doing the hardest job in the whole world -
because it is the most important. Well done.

Andrea Chatten Msc, MBPsS, PGCLandM, Bed(Hons), Dip.CBT

Andrea has been a specialised teacher for over 25 years, working with children from ages 5-16 with emotional and behavioural difficulties.

She is currently working as 'Lead Children's Emotional and Behavioural Psychologist' at Unravel CEBPC primarily with schools and families in and around the Sheffield area.

Developing positive, trusting relationships has always been at the heart of her practice with children and young people in order to nudge them into improved psychological well-being. Over the years, Andrea has developed and applied many positive developmental psychology approaches.

This insight is incorporated into her stories in order to help children, young people and their families to gain more of an understanding and potential strategies to try, in order to deal with a range of behavioural issues that children and young people might experience.

Andrea created "The Blinks" so that parents and carers could also benefit from reading the books with their children, particularly if they can identify with the children in the stories, and their own family circumstances. Both parent or carer and child could learn how to manage early forms of psychological distress as a natural part of growing up rather than it become problematic when not addressed in its early stages.

"The Blinks" is a series of books that discreetly apply lots of psychological theory throughout the stories including, Cognitive Behavioural Therapy, Developmental and Positive Psychology approaches.

This first book in the series tackles the issue of worry and how to prevent this everyday cognition from becoming more serious anxiety in the future.

Introduction

'The Blinks' books have been created to help children, young people and their families understand emotional and behavioural issues. They aim to provide strategies and techniques to help manage and change the intensity and duration of problematic behaviours over time. In this, the first book in 'The Blinks' series – 'Worry', the story is focussed on Amanda, who has always been a worrier. Over recent months, she has noticed that her worrying temperament has begun to impact negatively on other aspects of her life. These include her friendships, sleep, health and her ability to concentrate and learn at school.

At this stage of worrying, due to severity of the effect it is having on several important areas of her life, the length of time Amanda has been experiencing it, and the impact it is having on the quality of her life, her worrying could be regarded as problematic. It is also progressing towards becoming disordered. For the situation to improve, it would be helpful for Amanda to gain some understanding about what she is experiencing. It could also be valuable for her to learn some tools to help her take positive action in overcoming her worrying. This combination of insight + action is suggested to be the most positive formula to develop success and positive behaviour change.

Understanding/ Insight	+	Strategies/effort/ action	=	Success/ Positive change/ Happier children and young people

This book aims to help you, whether you are a parent, carer, older sibling, teacher or professional to understand the theory behind 'The Blinks' interventions. Then, if ever needed in the future, could be used to continue the work of 'The Blinks' with your loved ones too.

Section 1 - <u>Understanding the Psychology of Worry and Anxiety</u>

Worrying is normal and every human being experiences worrying thoughts throughout their lifetime. In many situations worry could be seen to be a useful exercise that allows us time to reflect on the reality of the situation which has triggered our thoughts of worry or concern. When we use solution focussed thinking, we use the time to reflect to come up with possibilities and outcomes that contribute to feelings of empowerment in order to take positive steps to rectify the worrying situation.

By doing what we feel is the most appropriate course of action, this helps to reduce the situation causing us the distress. For most people, most of the time, this is what we are doing with regard to managing our worries. However, we can all experience times when our thoughts become hijacked and our worrying becomes more extreme. Factors such as the amount of time we spend thinking, or the introduction of negative/irrational thought patterns can leave us feeling overwhelmed, out of control, and helpless. This may result in a period of intense worry or anxiety. Just to clarify, worry is the thought, anxiety is the feeling. By recognising that as adults, we can feel this from time to time, we can understand more how a child could be feeling However, to get to the true context we need to multiply by ten at least!

Worry is based on emotions and behaviours, and on the apprehension of future events. This leads to the onset of a bombardment of 'what if' questions. If left unanswered or challenged, these can cause a child or young person to experience a period of deep uncertainty, in turn leading them to feel vulnerable and fearful of their ability to cope. However it is important to remember that thoughts are in fact just guesses and so not attach ourselves to them too much. Thoughts need to be fluid, to come and go. It is also necessary as parents and carers that we actively listen to what our children are saying.

Listening or active listening is not the same as hearing, in that we do not fully concentrate on the dialogue but instead hear the words without engaging in the sounds. Active listening means that we put everything down, give full eye contact and listen wholeheartedly to what our children are saying. This helps us hear fully and make links with the deeper issues that children might not be verbalising. This skill becomes easier and more attuned if we are truly engaged and connected with our child's communication at that time.

It is also very important never to dismiss what a child or young person is worrying about, as this can contribute to the anxiety further. It can make them feel little and stupid and could lead them to holding these issues inside for longer and/or scared to say them out loud at all.

In my work as a Counsellor for ChildLine, a national charity, the taught philosophy is that "if it is a big problem to the child then it is a big problem to the listener". This approach reduces any judgement or bias to the situation and instead offers non-judgemental listening and genuine positive regard to each individual who phones in. By applying this to our children, we instantly make them feel valid in what they are feeling and confident that we are there for them.

This depth of relationship helps us guide children in how to understand worries and challenge them to find out whether they are useless worries or helpful thoughts. Any child who feels judged during this process will be more likely to feel that you are challenging them, and not what they are worrying about. This could lead to further withdrawal behaviours or worse, strong feelings of frustration and anger.

Useless worries and helpful thoughts – understanding the difference

Useless worries tend to be negative and irrational thoughts, the reality being that these would be more difficult or impossible to solve, or are more extreme. Useless thoughts are more likely to make children feel highly anxious and in this situation, it is important to help children recognise that not all feelings are facts. We can help our children find evidence to support or counteract why it may not be very helpful to think that way about that situation. An example of a child's useless thought might be 'what if none of my friends want to come to my birthday party?'

In this situation, we can work with our children to find all the rational reasons as to why this is unlikely to happen. All your friends like you, they've always come to your other parties and kids love parties, you haven't fallen out with them. Some might not be able to come but they will be sad to miss out on your great party. It doesn't mean that they don't like you. Providing valid evidence helps children understand how our brains can sometimes activate 'what if' questions, but that we all need to learn to question and challenge these whenever possible rather than leave them unanswered.

Helpful worries, on the other hand, are those which can motivate us to take positive action, for example, 'what if I don't do well in my spelling test?' Children can think about what they could or couldn't do to pass or fail the test. If they choose not to learn the spellings, then they are likely to not do too well. However, if they choose to learn their spellings, there is more chance that they will do okay. This could be regarded as a helpful worry as there is something pro-active that can be done to eliminate it.

How worry affects behavioural changes

It is also important that we, as parents, carers and teachers learn to recognise the behaviour changes in our children and learn to read them as signs of communication. Children who are pre-occupied with a worrying dialogue can present behaviours in many ways.

Some children and young people could withdraw socially and emotionally from those around them, almost shutting down, trying to process all that is going on in their brains at that difficult time. Some may become fearful of situations that may not normally be regarded as risky or threatening. It's more likely that these children will feel tearful, whilst others may engage in 'proximity seeking behaviours' or 'clinginess', wanting and needing to know that someone is there as a secure base during this time of perceived vulnerability.

It is also common for children to become 'short-fused' and 'ratty' during this difficult time. This is a sign that children are struggling to cope with all that they are feeling. This can lead children to overreact more rapidly due to their baseline of reasonableness having been nudged closer to crisis point reactions.

Children who worry or are anxious are also more likely to be highly perceptive to how you are feeling and how you are coping with their distress too. If you feel tense, stressed or anxious about our child's worrying state of mind, it's more likely that they will worry more, as the security and calming strength that they need from you is weakened.

As best as you can, try and recognise that what your child is going through is normal and can be supported positively with the tips that you will learn in this book. Remember you are the expert on your child so do what you feel is a good match to get the best outcome for your child.

However, it is also important to remember that very few changes happen overnight. It is therefore crucial to keep at it and practise the suggestions, not giving up until you feel confident that the concerning behaviour has made significant changes or improvement.

Worrying which has become problematic may have taken months, maybe years, to develop. It can therefore take time to understand it, break previous habits and try out and develop new ways to overcome the worrying rather than the worrying overcoming the child or young person.

Top tips for supporting issues of worry or anxiety

- Worry and anxiety are a normal responses to everyday life to help us solve problems or avoid dangerous situations. Worry and anxiety become disordered when they begin to interrupt a person's work or relationships due to the intensity and duration
- Worry and anxiety are best overcome by facing the irrational fears rather than avoiding them
- Avoiding fearful situations allows the worry and anxiety to grow and feel stronger
- Don't let the worry or anxiety become settled, the sooner fears are challenged the sooner they will improve
- Practise positive self-talk and question exaggerated worries (useless worry or helpful thought). This can really help to change bias, irrational thinking and divert and reduce negative dialogues
- Practise relaxation breathing techniques to reduce physical symptoms for example 7/11 breathing (breathe in for 7 seconds and slowly breathe out for 11 seconds). Or 4/7/8 breathing (breathe in for 4 seconds, hold for 7 seconds and breathe out slowly for 8 seconds). Both of these techniques act as a distraction to worry and anxiety, but also support as an act of mindfulness (being actively engaged in the present and stopping any negative thought processes at that

time). They also boost oxygen levels in the blood which activates the calming part of the brain, helping your child feel more in control

Questions for discussion with children and young people

1. Why do you think Amanda worries so much?
2. Do you know anyone who worries a lot like Amanda?
3. Write down all the things that you worry about, or do a 'what if' list.
4. How many things on your list would you call a useless worry? Talk about them and cross them out.
5. How many things on your list are helpful thoughts? Tick them and write down what you could do to stop yourself worrying about them.
6. If you were Blink Will Worry-Less, what advice would you give to Amanda?

Section 2 - <u>Cognitive Behavioural Therapy (CBT) approaches to support worry and anxiety</u>

CBT is a psychological practice that helps us recognise the impact of our thoughts and how they affect how we feel and fundamentally, what we believe. The main principles of CBT are that if we think something for long enough we will eventually feel it. The longer we feel it, the more likely we are to believe it.

In the book 'Worry', Amanda starts to think that she is stupid because of her worrying. Should Amanda have continued to engage in this thought process frequently and over a prolonged period of time, she would have started to feel stupid. This, in turn, would have begun to impact negatively on her self-confidence and also her self-esteem, particularly if she were beginning to believe that she was stupid.

What I think is how I feel!

An important component of Cognitive Behavioral Therapy and positive psychology is recognising how our thoughts affect how we feel and in turn what we believe about ourselves and the world in which we live. The diagram below helps us to understand how each phase feeds into the next.

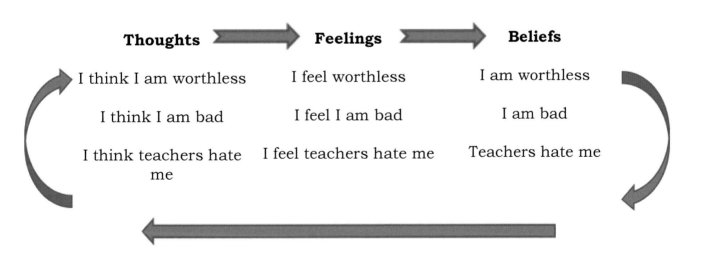

Thoughts	Feelings	Beliefs
I think I am worthless	I feel worthless	I am worthless
I think I am bad	I feel I am bad	I am bad
I think teachers hate me	I feel teachers hate me	Teachers hate me

It is important for us to realise that these negative thoughts and the amount of attention that we give to them cause them to grow in intensity and severity. One of the many wonderful things about the human brain is that it has unlimited scope for change due to the amazing plasticity of its function. We can change our beliefs by challenging them, or introducing new, positive thoughts. If we interrupt the negative self-talk, start being kinder with our thinking, or distracting ourselves in order to reduce the intensity, our thoughts, feelings and beliefs can also change over time. They become psychologically healthier, which increases feelings of happiness.

As parents and carers, it is important that we recognise that our thoughts, feelings and belief cycle can lead to positive and negative behaviours. Any children and young people who are presenting with challenging behaviours are likely to have an undercurrent of negative thoughts that drive their negative behaviour choices. Engaging in positive dialogue with a young person even when they are being most difficult, can divert the negative thought cycle which could be hijacking their cognitions and rational thoughts at that time.

Pressurised language and how it impacts on worry and anxiety

Many children's and young people's thoughts are dominated by a high level of negative mental chatter which research suggests can be as much as 12,000 words a minute during times of severe worry or distress. This cognitive thought process can also be driven with overtly high expectations of what children and young people think they **'should'** be doing or being, which puts an alarming pressure on their day to day life.

This negative **'should'** talk feeds into negative comparisons to other people, other lifestyles and hence sets unrealistic expectations of oneself. As you can imagine, this is not only exhausting but also extremely damaging to self-esteem. In the long term children who feel that they are never good enough, never doing things well enough or never feel worthy, experience feelings of lowered self-esteem. This can activate the internal pressure even more to be better at driving the negative comparisons further.

It is important to help young people understand the damage that **'should'** vocabulary can do. By working on changing **'shoulds'** to **_'coulds'_** , the child or young person has a choice which instantly removes the feeling of being pressured or forced into things that they do.

Rather than thinking "I **'should'** be better behaved" which leaves a feeling of inferiority and failure, teach your child to think "I **_'could'_** be better behaved." This subtle shift enables children and young people to see that there are options, and options they can choose to try. This not only supports emotional development but also fosters resilience.

As parents and carers, we are fundamental in helping children and young people who present with similar issues make positive changes. Our role can not only guide and nudge development but also consolidate this valuable process, to aid their emotional and psychological well-being across the lifespan.

Top tips to reduce negative self-talk dialogues

- See negative behaviour as a mirror to the child or young person's perceptions of either themselves or the situation. This knowledge can help us to respond with greater compassion even in the most extreme situations
- When a child or young person is behaving in a way that is inappropriate, make it very clear what you want from them and why. However, it is also hugely important to remind them that you see them as better than the behaviour that they are presenting. Children with emotional and behavioural issues need to be reminded that your expectations of them are high not low
- Challenge negative thinking whenever you hear it. Young people can make progress from having an understanding and some insight into what it is that they are experiencing. By helping children and young people understand the process, we can guide them through a journey of self-discovery and autonomy
- If children and young people appear to be engaging in negative self-talk, suggest that they distract those thoughts or reduce the amount of time they spend engaging with them
- Recommend that young people engage in positive self-dialogue to offset the negativity

Questions for discussion with children and young people

1. Do you have any regular negative thoughts? Write them down or talk about them.

2. Can you think of any times when you use the word 'should' with yourself?

3. Write down 3 things that you need to do. Write them down as 'shoulds' and then turn them to 'coulds'. How does each sentence make you feel? Discuss.

Section 3- <u>**How worry and anxiety impacts on Self-esteem**</u>

Self-esteem is how much we know, like and love ourselves, and is fundamental to everything that we do. If we believe that we are loveable, then we are more likely to develop more meaningful relationships and aspire to achieve. If we do not like who we are then it can hinder these areas and more.

As mentioned earlier, when children feel that they are pre-occupied with negative thoughts and do not feel that they are capable of making appropriate choices, they can begin to question who they are, whether they are good enough and how capable they are. Many children think that if they are doing something badly, or make 'bad' choices regularly, then they are 'bad' people. It is the activation of this process that can have the most damaging effect on how a child feels about themselves over time (thoughts=feelings=beliefs).

The other issue for children whose self-esteem is lower is that they could be less likely to seek support as they do not feel worthy of your time. By trusting your instincts, being perceptive to any changes in your child's mood or behaviours and making talking a natural part of your relationship, these longer term issues of lowered self-esteem can be reduced, as you invest into their self-esteem pot.

The fuller their pot of feel good feelings becomes, the happier each child feels about who they are which again further supports emotional development. It is also very important that whilst tackling worrying issues, to help children to understand that worrying is okay, normal and that we all do it sometimes. However, children need to understand that they have their own individual power and control to change it if they desire.

<u>*Questions and tasks for discussion with children and young people*</u>

1. What does self-esteem mean?
2. Write down 5 things that you like about yourself.
3. Write down 5 things that you think other people like about you.
4. Keep an achievement diary. Try and notice 5 things you do every day that makes you feel proud of what you did.
5. Start a happiness log. Try and notice 5 things a day that make you feel happy every day.

(Tasks 4 and 5 both support mindfulness by teaching children how to be in the moment and feel what we are experiencing. They also contribute to a child or young person's self-esteem pot.)

Section 4 - <u>**A bit about Emotional Development**</u>

Typically developing children more naturally progress through the different stages of emotional development and become confident, trusting, accepting young people who embrace diversity and become independent learners. However, emotional development involves many complex stages which can be hindered unconsciously with differing parenting approaches. For instance, a lack of understanding or ability to nurture to a child's emotional needs (which even in the best case scenario, research suggests we are only 30% accurate), and/or difficult life events can lead to us not being as emotionally available when our child might need us the most.

From the table below we can see how a child or young person with a worrying temperament and sensitive nature could require more support in the confirmation stage of who they are (Being Stage) and what they feel that they are capable of (Doing Stage).

STAGE	Gaps in emotional growth (non-typical development)	Affirmations needed from Parent/carer to child	Healthy emotional growth (typical development)
Being (birth - 6 months)	Developmental block = **Don't exist, don't be, don't trust** ❖ Withdrawn, nervous, scared of change ❖ Does not recognise own needs, does not call for care ❖ Repeated oral behaviours	Emotional need = **contact** ✓ I'm glad you are here ✓ You belong ✓ Your needs are important to me ✓ You can feel all of your feelings ✓ We want to care for you	❖ Confident and trusting ❖ Embraces new experiences and relationships ❖ Aware of own needs, signals any distress, asks for help

STAGE	Gaps in emotional growth (non-typical development)	Affirmations needed from Parent/carer to child	Healthy emotional growth (typical development)
Doing (6-18 months)	Developmental block = **don't be active, don't do**	Emotional need = **stimulus**	
	❖ Passive, quiet, holds back	✓ You can explore we will keep you safe	❖ Curious, creative, use their initiative
	❖ Struggles to settle and engage	✓ You can try things as many times as you need	❖ Active, easily stimulated, enjoy sensory experiences
	❖ Responds with extremes	✓ You can be interested in everything	❖ Enjoys being involved and experimenting
		✓ I love watching you grow and learn	

STAGE	Gaps in emotional growth (non-typical development)	Affirmations needed from Parent/carer to child	Healthy emotional growth (typical development)
Thinking (18 months - 3 years)	Developmental block = **don't think**	Emotional need = **structure**	
	❖ Oppositional to requests, acts strong and tough	✓ I am glad you are starting to think for yourself	❖ Can think, express and deal with emotions
	❖ Directive towards others	✓ You can say no and push the limits	❖ Understands cause and effect, basic rules
	❖ Demanding, pushy	✓ It's okay to be angry but I won't let you hurt yourself or others	❖ Can think for themselves and say no
	❖ Overreacts	✓ You can know what you need and ask for help	
	❖ Can feel a victim	✓ You can be yourself and I will still care for you	

STAGE	Gaps in emotional growth (non-typical development)	Affirmations needed from Parent/carer to child	Healthy emotional growth (typical development)
Identity & Power (3-6 years)	Developmental block = **don't be who you are, don't be you** ❖ Overpowering, threatening, bullying, lies ❖ Low self-confidence and self-esteem ❖ Boasts reputation to bolster identity	Emotional need = **recognition** ✓ You can explore who you are and find out about others ✓ You can try out different ways of using your power ✓ All of your feelings are ok ✓ You can learn from the results of your behaviour	❖ Sound sense of self and own identity ❖ Understands different roles and relationships ❖ Recognises actions, behaviours and consequences in context

STAGE	Gaps in emotional growth (non-typical development)	Affirmations needed from Parent/carer to child	Healthy emotional growth (typical development)
Skills & Structure (6-12 years)	Developmental block = **don't make mistakes** ❖ Struggles with authority and rules ❖ Mismatch between expectations and skills ❖ Very laid back, over casual ❖ Does not finish tasks	Emotional need = **excitement, frequency** ✓ It is okay to stop and think before you respond with yes and no ✓ Mistakes are good, they mean that you are learning ✓ You can trust your instinct to decide what to do ✓ You can find ways of doing things that are good for you ✓ You can learn when and how to disagree ✓ You can decide when to get help rather than stay distressed ✓ We always want to be with you and it is okay to differ, that is when we can learn more about each other together	❖ Embraces diversity and difference ❖ Recognises own internal/external structure of values/codes of conduct ❖ Identifies with same sex group

STAGE	Gaps in emotional growth (non-typical development)	Affirmations needed from Parent/carer to child	Healthy emotional growth (typical development)
Integration (Separation and Sexuality) (12-18 years)	Developmental block = **don't grow up** ❖ Engages in inappropriate risk-taking behaviours ❖ Poor relationships ❖ Struggles to separate	Emotional need = **sex, freedom** ✓ You can know who you are and learn / practise skills for being independent ✓ You can develop your own relationships and interests ✓ You can grow and develop in your gender role, but it is okay to still need help ✓ You can adapt old skills to create new ways ✓ We are excited by who you will become as an adult ✓ We trust that you will ask for support when you need it	❖ Enjoys being who they are ❖ Embraces independence ❖ Develops a confident sexual identity ❖ Engages in challenges and new experiences

This table reinforces the Cycle of Development model produced by Levin (1982), explaining how typically developing children mature emotionally when compared to non-typically developing children. Children need positive affirmations (messages from us through words and actions), opportunities and nurturing support to successfully complete these stages which can be a challenge for them and parents.

This process begins from birth and matures across the lifespan to age 18. However, the first 5 stages occur between the ages of 0 and 12 years. From the table, you will recognise how some children and young people can become developmentally blocked in various stages along the way. The 'Identity & Power' stage, from experience, is the most common area that children get stuck and which typically occurs between the areas of 3 and 6 years, though I know many 14-year-old boys who are still presenting in this stage and experiencing many emotional and behavioural difficulties, as you can imagine.

It becomes apparent that age isn't a number for many of our children, it is a state of mind. The 'Affirmations' section of the table supports the part that we, as parents and carers can do to support the emotional development of our children. As this is a cycle, it is possible to revisit areas that may need some extra input to continue the developmental process. It is recommended, however, that to always revisit the stage prior to the phase that you feel your child may be presenting with, to ensure to maximise the benefit and progress.

Hindered emotional development can also negatively impact on many other psychological concepts including moral reasoning and self-regulation. Children and young people are highly perceptive. When they feel that they are not making the right choices, like their typically developing peers, they will feel a sense of sadness and failure. This also damages self-esteem and their ability to bounce back after events (resilience), which highlights how important this area of development is for children's and young people's engagement in learning and more importantly quality of life across the lifespan.

Top tips to support healthy emotional development

- Apply a nurturing ethos at home
- Listen to children and young people without judgement
- Start small – choose one or two affirmations that you feel comfortable with and see how it goes
- If you think that your child is in the 'Identity and Power Stage' go back a stage and start with the 'Thinking Stage'
- Ask rather than tell
- Reiterate do's rather than don'ts
- Be very clear about instructions and sanctions as this allows children and young people 'take up' time to process what will happen either way and so supporting correct behaviour choices
- Celebrate mistakes as part of the learning process and use them to educate when possible even when applying sanctions
- Use language carefully "I don't care about why you were late" to a child means "I don't care about you"
- Find the good whenever you can and praise as much as possible
- Keep your expectations high and nudge them towards the behaviour that you require through positive modelling
- Remember that young people rarely remember what you say but they will never forget how you make them feel

Summary

This reference manual has hopefully provided some key psychological theory that will help with understanding beneficial ways to support a child who has developed a worrying nature or temperament. It is crucial that parents, carers, teachers and anyone who is actively engaged in the child or young person's life, support with calmness and reassurance.

Children and young people who worry, are also hyper-vigilant to other peoples' worries and anxieties, which can understandably make the situation worse for them and for you. Reiterate often that what they are experiencing is normal and that with some effort they can become hopeful that things will change for the better.

Worry - Summary Checklist – little things that can help in a big way!

- Make talking a normal part of your relationship with your child. It will always seem awkward at the start but practise makes perfect
- Trust your instincts and gut reaction. If you think something is wrong, you are probably right. Ask your child or young person gently if everything is okay as you had noticed that they were maybe not being themselves. It's important that if your child does not feel ready to speak there and then it is not a rejection of you. They just need to think about how to start putting these thoughts and feelings into words. Remind them that you love them and that you are here whenever they are ready. Make sure that you check in regularly asking them how they are and that you are always there until they are ready to share something that for them could be very difficult to say out loud
- Listen actively so that your child feels they have your full attention and so that you can pick up any underlying issues that the child may be trying to communicate
- Help your child understand the difference between helpful worries and useful thoughts
- Use a script or mantra to help offset negative thinking and introduce a positive thought dialogue that will not only distract from negative thinking, but more so activate rational evidence, for example, "I am safe, I am loved, I am protected".
- Remember worry is the thought, anxiety is the feeling
- Do not pander to worries or give in to them as this makes useless thoughts feel valid and reinforces that the worry is real and in charge. If your child is worried about going to school because of a fall out with a friend that has led to a series of negative 'what ifs', for example, 'What if the person has an argument with me? What if they are unkind? What if they get other people to not be my friend? What if no one likes me anymore? What if I have no one to play at playtime? Each one of these 'what ifs' feels huge to the child in question and we need to

work through each one so that they see the situation more rationally. This will leave your child feeling more able to cope with the day ahead, but more so fosters inner strength and resilience when they face up to their worry rather than give in to it

- Worries are guesses. Try not to fuse to them, let them come and go
- Try to reduce pressurised language like '*should*', '*need to*', '*always*', etc. as this makes children feel that it is a **must** rather than a choice. Instead, try changing '*shoulds*' to '*coulds*' as this makes the child feel like there is a choice, for example, they could do their homework now, or they could make better behaviour choices at school
- Be patient. Emotional and behavioural change takes time. However with insight and by practising the suggestions made by 'The Blinks', you are more likely to experience the positive change that you desire
- If you feel that your child's worrying is becoming increasingly problematic and they do not appear to be engaging in the process, refer your child or young person to your GP so that a psychological assessment can be carried out if necessary. Also, speak to your child's class teacher or school SENCO for advice and a possible Educational Psychologist or Behavioural Psychologist assessment and intervention programme

Finally, if you and your child have enjoyed 'The Blinks' – Worry – novel (the first in this engaging new series) then look out for 'The Blinks' – Anger.

To get in touch on social media please go to:
Facebook - /Theblinksbooks
Twitter - @BlinksThe

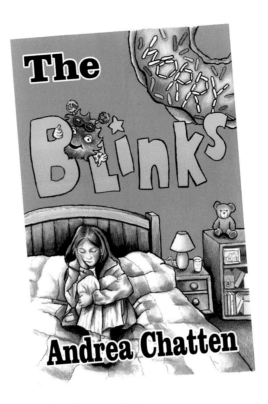

A magical novel for 7-11 year olds'

'The Blinks' are created from morsels of goodness, that all the good folk who have ever lived leave to the Universe. Their whole purpose is to share their wisdom and kindness with children.

When Amanda is discussed at the midnight meeting she is lucky to become part of some very special Blink intervention. As a result Amanda begins to make changes she never thought possible.

Read more and order at www.oodlebooks.com and www.theblinks.co.uk.
Also available on Amazon and Kindle.

Other titles in the series: